Father Junípero Serra

A Proud Heritage The Hispanic Library

Father Junípero Serra

and the California Missions

Sarah Bowler

The
Child's
World

Chapter One

From Old Spain to New Spain

"Always go forward. Never go back."

This simple motto, found in Junípero Serra's writings, describes his life. Born on a simple farm, he went on to become a famous priest. He traveled far from his home to the Americas to help settle California. He never went back, even after he was crippled from a mysterious bite. He walked thousands of miles to build a string of frontier **missions.** He never went back, even when Native Americans attacked his missions.

Junípero Serra was born on November 24, 1713, in a village on the Spanish island of Majorca. He was so tiny and frail that his parents were afraid he would die. They rushed to have him **baptized** so he would be a Christian if he died. He would always be small but lived for 70 years.

Margarita and Antonio Serra named their son Miguel José. As a boy, Miguel carried water from the town well.

He also collected firewood and helped on the family farm. Miguel was often sick. His mother told him to ignore his illnesses. She said he should get up and go outdoors as soon as he could. This attitude helped him through a life filled with illness and hardship.

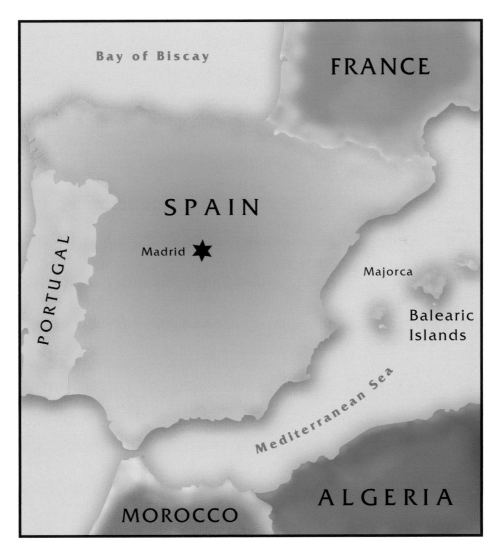

Junípero Serra was born in Spain on the island of Majorca.

A Priestly Path

Although his parents could not read or write, they wanted Miguel to be educated. When he was only 14, he went to the university in Palma, Majorca's biggest city. He decided to study to become a Franciscan priest. He could not sing in the choir, though, because he was too short to turn the pages of the hymnbook!

After years of study, Miguel took the vows to become a priest. It was the custom to take a new name at this time. Miguel chose the name Junípero. He was now 27 years old and had reached his full height of five feet, two inches (157 centimeters).

Father Serra studied and taught in Palma for the next 18 years. One of his first students was Francisco Palóu, who would later work with him in California. Serra also preached in local churches. People loved his deep voice and stirring **sermons.**

Serra dreamed of going to the Americas as a **missionary.** Spain had been sending missionaries to the Americas since the early 1500s. Their job was to **convert** the Native Americans to the Roman Catholic religion. They also tried to teach them how to live like Spaniards. Father Serra's superiors didn't want to lose such an excellent teacher. It was many years before they allowed him to go to Mexico, which was then a Spanish colony called New Spain. He knew he would never see his family again.

Far from Home

Father Serra was 36 years old when he sailed across the Atlantic in 1749. His friend, Father Palóu, was with him. The crowded, creaky ship rocked violently in the stormy sea. There wasn't enough food and water. The crew and passengers were seasick and thirsty. Father Serra wrote that some-

Serra left his home in Spain in 1749.

times he was so thirsty he "would have drunk slime." He never complained though.

After more than four months, the ship reached Veracruz. Father Serra still had to get to Mexico City more than 250 miles (400 kilometers) away. Mules had been sent to carry the priests, but they had not yet arrived. Father Serra did not want to wait. To show his devotion to God, he decided to walk the entire way.

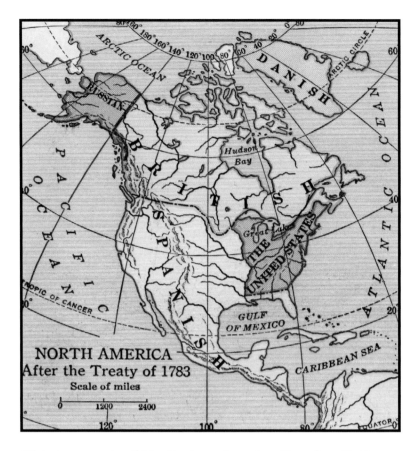

This is a map of North America shortly after Father Serra died. Notice that New Spain is much larger than the area that had just won its independence from England and become the United States.

He set out with another priest. They walked about 20 miles (32 kilometers) a day, over mountains and through forests. They ate what they found along the way. One night in the jungle, something bit Father Serra on the leg. The next day the bite was an open sore. His leg had swollen to almost twice its normal size. He could hardly walk, but he insisted they go on. That little bite would leave him crippled for the rest of his life.

In Mexico City, Father Serra took classes to learn how to teach Native Americans about Christianity. Catholic priests had been starting missions in Mexico for 200 years. Father Serra's first assignment was in one of these missions in the rugged mountains north of Mexico City.

The Old Basilica in Mexico City existed when Serra arrived there. It was built on the site where a Christian Aztec named Juan Diego claimed to have seen the Virgin Mary in 1531.

Father Serra and Father Palóu went to work with the Pame (PAH-may) Indians. They taught them to grow food and take care of sheep and goats. The women learned to make baskets to sell at the market. Many Pames converted to Christianity, and soon they had to build a bigger church. Father Serra stayed at this mission for eight years.

The Americas were new to Europeans. But Native Americans had been living in Alta California for many centuries before the Spanish arrived. By the time Father Serra came, there were about 72,000 people from more than 100 tribes living in Alta California. Customs and languages varied among the tribes, but they shared some common traits.

Many of their houses were made of sticks and reeds, with a smoke hole in the roof. When the hut became dirty, they would burn it and build another. They didn't need many clothes. Men and children mostly went naked. Women wore skirts made of shredded bark or deerskin.

They ate what nature provided. The men hunted and fished. The women gathered nuts, seeds, and berries. They made flour by crushing acorns. There was plenty of food, and they only took what they needed.

When people had problems, a **council of elders** discussed them. They voted on important decisions. Storytellers passed the traditions on to the children. Medicine men cured the sick. They believed in a Great Spirit that was part of everything. The whole village attended ceremonies and rituals that celebrated the cycle of the seasons.

These people did not move from place to place. They were settled, organized societies when the Spanish came to change their lives forever.

Then he was called back to Mexico City. During the next nine years he traveled more than 5,000 miles (8,050 kilometers), preaching to the natives. He also became well known for his sermons in Mexico City. Sometimes the wealthy Spanish women came to church just to talk to their friends. They might have their servants bring them chocolate to drink. They didn't like it when Father Serra spoke out against their behavior.

Even Farther from Home

In 1767, Father Serra was placed in charge of the 15 missions already established in Baja California. *Baja* means "below" in Spanish. Baja California is still the name for the long, narrow **peninsula** that runs from California along the western side of Mexico. He worked there for one year. Then Spain decided to send Father Serra into new territory.

In the 1500s and 1600s, a few Spanish explorers sailed up the coast of Alta (upper) California, as it was known in those days. Spain had claimed the region but then ignored it for 150 years—until Russian fur traders started moving south from Alaska. King Carlos III of Spain felt his territories were threatened. He decided to send missionaries to Alta California. They would start a chain of missions to show that Spain controlled the area. Father Serra was chosen for the job.

Chapter Two

A Man on a Mission

Father Serra was ready to go forward again. He had a lot of work to do. He walked hundreds of miles gathering items for the trip. There were holy objects for the churches they would build, including paintings of saints and 18 bells. They also packed tools, pots, blankets, and seeds. They needed 163 mules to carry the supplies.

The plan was to send three ships from La Paz, at the southern end of Baja California. Two land expeditions would leave from Santa Maria, a mission settlement to the north. The five groups were to meet in San Diego. Father Serra was to travel with the second overland group, led by Gaspar de Portolá. Father Serra was already exhausted, and his leg was painfully swollen. Portolá thought he might not survive the difficult journey ahead. He asked Father Serra to wait and come later. But Father Serra would not be left behind.

A Difficult Journey

Portolá's party set out in the spring of 1769. There were more than 50 men—soldiers, Christian Native Americans, and Father Serra. They also brought cattle and pack mules. One day Father Serra asked the men who took care of the mules for some of the ointment that they used on the animals. They laughed, but they made up the medicine from herbs and grease. Father Serra tried it and it worked! His leg felt much better.

Father Serra is still a well-known and highly honored historical figure in California.

The trip was difficult. The men stumbled and fell on the rugged trail. Everyone slept on the ground. Sometimes the roars of mountain lions kept them awake. They could not always find clean water, and food supplies were short. Many of the converts ran away in the night.

As they traveled north, the land changed. Instead of the parched desert, they saw lush green trees. The party had been traveling for more than three months. At last they saw the ocean. In the distance they saw the sails of two ships!

When the boats docked, Father Serra and his men were shocked by what they saw. The sailors were desperately thin and weak, with missing teeth and bleeding gums. They had a disease called scurvy that was caused by a lack of fresh fruit and vegetables.

Father Serra and the others who were well enough made tents out of the ships' sails. There they cared for the sick men. Only half of the 300 men who had left for San Diego were still alive. Many more would die in the following weeks. The third ship was never heard from again.

One of the ships, the *San Antonio,* was immediately sent back to Mexico for more men and supplies. Two weeks later, Portolá took a group of men to try to find Monterey Bay. The plan was to build the first mission at San Diego and the second one at Monterey. Then they would build the other missions between these two points.

The First Mission

After they left, Father Serra put up a wooden cross to mark the site of the first California mission, San Diego de Alcalá. He hung a bell on a nearby tree and called the men to Mass, the most important service in the Catholic religion.

Then they began building simple huts out of branches and small trees. One was the church, and the others were used for living quarters and supply sheds. Father Serra also planted a garden.

As they worked, they saw Native Americans watching them. Father Serra gave them beads and ribbons and showed them the new church. Some Native Americans were curious. Others were hostile.

Mission San Diego de Alcalá was Father Serra's first mission in California. It was built in 1769.

One night, a group of Native Americans cut the ship's sails and stole things. Another time, an angry group attacked the mission, wounding many Spaniards with bows and arrows. The Native Americans quickly ran away when they heard the soldiers' guns.

The soldiers wanted to punish the Native Americans, but Father Serra refused to let them. Instead, he treated wounded Native Americans who came back to the mission. After this incident, more Native Americans came around to help with the building. Sometimes they ate meals with the priests. Still, Father Serra did not convert anyone for more than a year.

There were other problems. The Spanish did not know how to fish, hunt, and gather food. The garden had not had time to produce. The supply ship had not arrived from Mexico. The people were starving. Making matters worse, many people came down with scurvy.

For six months there was no word from Portolá. When he finally returned, he had bad news. His group had run out of food. Portolá reported that he had not been able to find Monterey. He had left a wooden cross at a bay, but the spot didn't match an earlier explorer's description of Monterey.

When Portolá saw how bad conditions were at the mission, he wanted to take everybody back to Mexico. Father Serra said he would not go back. He pleaded with the soldiers to wait until March 19. Portolá agreed to stay until then. The priests prayed.

On March 19, the soldiers prepared for the long ride south. Then, in the distance, a small sail appeared. It was the *San Antonio!* Father Serra was overjoyed. The missions would now go forward.

Chapter Three

Success despite Hardship

Father Serra and Portolá planned another expedition to search for Monterey. This time Father Serra would sail on the *San Antonio*. Portolá would go by land with 12 soldiers. Two other priests and a few soldiers would stay at the San Diego mission.

The two groups left San Diego in the middle of April 1770. After six weeks, the land party reached the bay where they had left the cross. Portolá looked again at the bay and decided that it must be Monterey after all. The description from the earlier explorer had been made from the sea and during a different season. Perhaps the explorer had exaggerated his discovery to please the king.

The *San Antonio* was sighted a week later. Portolá's men lit fires on the beach to guide the ship into the bay. On June 3, 1770, the Native Americans watched as two **processions** walked toward an altar in the woods. One

In this painting of the presidio in San Francisco, you can see both Native Americans and Spaniards.

group came from the sea and another came from the land. Father Serra, dressed in purple robes, said the Mass. The northern mission was established. Portolá returned to Mexico City, where there was a celebration.

The priest and the soldiers got busy building the new mission and a **presidio,** or fort. Some of the local Native Americans helped. They finished the first buildings in about a month.

Although the work went well, there were problems. A soldier named Pedro Fages was now in charge of the Spanish settlements in Alta California. Many of the soldiers deserted because he treated them so badly. He was even worse with the Native Americans. He beat them for minor mistakes. If they ran away, he caught them and had them whipped. The priests knew that this would make it hard to win their trust.

The Mission at Carmel

Father Serra decided to move the mission away from the presidio and the soldiers. He found a beautiful spot about 5 miles (8 kilometers) away on the bay of Carmel. It had a beautiful river, good soil, and lots of tall trees. The carpenters built a new church and rooms for the priests. Father Serra decorated the church with the items he had brought from Baja. He put silver candlesticks on the altar and hung a picture of the Virgin Mary on the wall. He named the mission San Carlos Borromeo de Carmelo.

The picture on the left shows the gate at the Carmel mission. The one on the right shows the covered walkway at the mission at Santa Barbara. These features are typical of Spanish-built missions.

Many Native Americans from a nearby village began to come to the early morning prayers. There is no way of knowing what made them come to the mission. It might have been the music or the prayers or the hot bowls of cereal.

Father Serra worked hard to learn the Native Americans' language. He also tried to teach them Spanish. He made clothes for the children so they would not be naked. A few Native Americans were baptized and moved into the mission. Father Serra liked the area so much that he made this mission his headquarters.

Again food supplies began to run low. It had been a year since the last supply ship had come. There was not enough food to feed the settlers and the converts. This time Commander Fages came to the rescue. He organized a bear hunt to get meat for the mission.

When the ship finally came, it brought supplies and ten new missionaries. Father Serra was excited about being able to start new missions. He decided to post two priests at each one so they wouldn't get lonely.

Moving Inland

Most of the missions were to be established on the coast. There the supplies from the ships could easily get to them. But Father Serra wanted to reach inland villages as well.

He took two missionaries into the mountains south of Monterey. They found a valley with tall trees and wild grape-vines. After they unpacked the mules, Father Serra hung a bell on a tree limb. He rang it to announce the founding of Mission San Antonio de Pádua.

Soon a few members of the Salinan tribe brought nuts and seeds for the Spanish visitors. In the days that followed, they helped with the building of the church. One of the fathers, Father Sitjar, ended up staying for 37 years. He wrote

Mission San Antonio de Pádua was the first inland mission.

a 400-page vocabulary book of the Salinan language.

Father Serra went on to start a mission in the valley where the soldiers had hunted the bears. He named it Mission San Luis Obispo de Tolosa. A supply ship came just in time with lumber to build the chapel.

The next mission was San Gabriel Arcángel. Again Father Serra chose a place where there were many Native Americans. There was trouble at San Gabriel almost from

This old drawing of Mission San Luis Rey shows the field workers, their huts, and the mission church.

the beginning. The soldiers assaulted the Indian women and beat or killed anyone who tried to stop them. Very few Native Americans wanted to come to the mission after that.

When he heard what was happening at San Gabriel, Father Serra was very angry. He complained to Fages, who refused to punish the soldiers. Fages said that the missions would fail because the "childlike" Native Americans were not capable of understanding the Catholic religion. He suggested the Spanish should instead use the Native Americans to build roads and forts.

Father Serra decided he needed to speak to the viceroy about these problems. The viceroy was in charge of all the Spanish territory in the Americas. Father Serra sailed on a supply ship and then walked to Mexico City to see him.

Each mission was built about a day's walk from the last one. That way, the priests didn't have to go far if they needed help. Also, weary travelers would always have a place to stop for the night.

Mission life followed a strict schedule. Converts awoke early to the tolling of bells. They attended services and ate breakfast, which was usually hot cereal made of corn. Then the day's work began. The converts were trained in a variety of skills. The men learned to make furniture, saddles, and wagons and do stonework. The women learned to make candles and soap, weave cloth, and sew clothing. They also made wine and olive oil. Both men and women helped in the fields and orchards.

At lunchtime the bells rang again. After lunch everyone took a siesta, or nap. Then they would go back to their work until the bells rang for 5 P.M. prayers. Dinner was at 6 P.M., followed by more instruction. They might learn about music, religious paintings, or the Spanish language. At bedtime, the converts who lived in the mission were locked in their rooms until morning.

There were few breaks in the routine. Sometimes, if there was a visitor, there might be a party, called a fiesta. Other times the Native Americans might be allowed to perform their traditional songs and dances. But on the whole, mission life was a strict schedule of hard work.

This painting shows Native Americans dancing at the San Francisco mission around 1815.

The new viceroy, Antonio Bucareli, listened carefully to Father Serra. He ordered many changes that were good for the missions. He removed Commander Fages. The priests were to have more control over the welfare of the Native Americans. Soldiers who abused them would lose their jobs. He agreed to send families and tradesmen to open a new northern settlement in the San Francisco area. Father Serra returned to Carmel pleased with the support he had won for the missions.

Chapter Four

The Foundations of a New Society

The families the viceroy sent to Alta California traveled 1,600 miles (2,570 kilometers). Some 240 people, many of them children, plodded over craggy mountains and through harsh deserts. They were in constant danger of being attacked by Apache Indians. Their heroic leader, Captain Juan Bautista de Anza, brought them safely to San Gabriel in six months.

After a few days of rest, the party pushed on to San Francisco. They traveled on the trail between the missions. It was now a good road, maintained by Native American converts. Father Serra called it *El Camino Real,* or "the Royal Highway."

They reached the great bay nearly five months later. The colonists, soldiers, and priests got to work. They built the *presidio,* the town, and the mission. When the mission was finished, Father Serra led a procession to the church. There he placed the statue of St. Francis on the altar. He named the mission San Francisco de Asis, in honor of St. Francis. He said the first Mass in the fall of 1776. That same year the American colonies declared their independence from Great Britain. Father Palóu was left in charge of the new mission.

Father Serra then returned to Carmel to face more problems. He had always had arguments with the military leaders. They disagreed on who had the right to make decisions about the missions. Now he felt that the new governor, Felipe de Neve, was keeping him from going forward.

Father Serra wanted to take a trip around the missions to **confirm** as many Native Americans as possible. Being confirmed is an important ceremony in becoming a Catholic. The Pope, the head of the Roman Catholic Church, had given Father Serra special permission to perform confirmations.

Governor Neve demanded to see the original letter from the Pope that gave this permission. Father Serra sent for the letter but didn't wait for it to arrive. He started on his tour, despite the governor's orders. He confirmed more than 1,700 Native Americans.

Governor Neve was angry but did not punish Father Serra. He knew he needed the priests to keep the missions

On the top is a bird's eye view of San Francisco in 1851. Today, San Francisco is a city of more than 700,000 people.

going and to build new ones. Around this time, the Spanish government made Monterey the capital of Alta California. Father Serra was proud that the government wanted his favorite mission to be the capital.

Again Father Serra was busy planning new missions. The first of these was San Juan Capistrano, founded in 1776. It was a beautiful mission surrounded by fields of wild roses. In 1777, he moved on to start Mission Santa Clara de Asis, near San Francisco.

In 1782, he founded San Buenaventura near a Chumash village of 500 people. It turned out to be his last mission. The military leaders prevented him from starting any others. They felt the missions were getting too powerful. Father Serra was disappointed, but he continued to help the other missions grow.

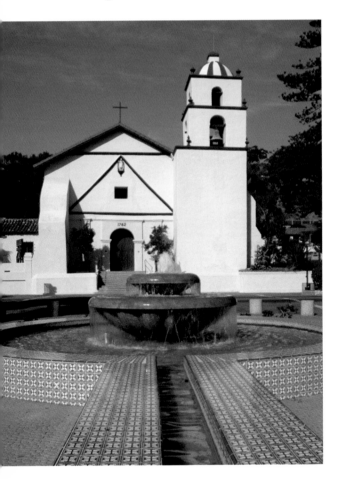

San Buenaventura Mission was the last mission established by Father Serra.

The Final Journey

In 1784, Father Serra was 70 years old. His bad leg had given him trouble throughout his years in Alta California. His lungs were so weak it was difficult for him to breathe. He decided to take a final journey to all of his missions. His followers built a stretcher with a seat on which to carry him, but he refused to use it. Instead he rode a mule or walked the hundreds of miles.

The missions were thriving. There were farms, work-shops, and schools. About 7,000 Native Americans had become Christians, and at every stop new ones asked to be baptized. Father Serra was pleased by what he saw.

When Father Serra returned to Carmel four months later, he told his friends that he had come home to die. He lived for a few more months.

One day before he died an Indian woman told him she was cold. He went to his room and came out with a piece of blanket. He had cut his only blanket in half to share with her.

Father Palóu came from San Francisco to be with Father Serra in his last days. Father Serra died on August 28, 1784, holding the cross he had brought from Spain. Hundreds of people—priests, converts, soldiers, and other colonists—came together for his funeral.

Serra's Legacy

"Always go forward. Never go back." Father Serra had lived up to his motto for 50 years. Nothing—not his constantly infected leg, problems with the soldiers, or poor health—had stopped him from going forward.

Under his direction, nine missions and three *presidios* had been established. Thousands of Native Americans who had become Christians were living and working at

These Mexican-American men on horses are called charros. *They are putting on a show outside of Mission San Gabriel to celebrate its 200th anniversary.*

the missions. He had taught them to grow food and many other new skills. Father Serra had no idea how much his work would influence modern-day California. Farming is one of the most important parts of the state's economy. The artichokes, almonds, figs, and apricots that are sold in California today were first grown on the missions. El Camino Real is still an important highway. Spanish architecture still exists throughout southern California. Thriving modern cities, such as San Francisco and San Diego, began as Father Serra's missions.

He came to the Americas to spread his religion. In the process, he brought knowledge and skills that served as a basis for a new society.

What about the Native Americans?

Few people could argue with Father Serra's courage and **dedication.** But many have questioned whether what he did was right. The story of Father Serra is based mostly on the writings of Father Palóu. It is told from the missionaries' perspective.

But what about the Native Americans' point of view? There are few, if any, records from Father Serra's time that tell how they felt. We know that many of the native people strongly resisted the change. Over the years there were many attacks on the missions.

The Spanish treated the Native Americans like children. Once they were baptized, they had to live at the missions. They could not visit their villages without permission or stay away for too long.

The fathers sometimes beat the converts for neglecting their duties. Whipping, a common form of punishment in Europe, was not part of Native American culture.

The drastic change in lifestyle took its toll. The Native Americans had been healthy people before the Spanish arrived. They were used to freedom, fresh air, and food from the land. After the Spanish came, they were locked into enclosed spaces, had to follow rigid schedules, and suffered from the diseases the Spanish brought. The Indian death rate increased sharply. The

These performers are reenacting mission life in Father Serra's time. They are portraying Serra and two Indian friends.

native population between San Francisco and San Diego dropped from 72,000 to 18,000 during the entire mission period.

The native culture was also largely lost. The Native Americans' spiritual beliefs were replaced by Christianity. Their social customs were changed or forgotten if they didn't fit into Spanish life. Even their Native American names were changed.

However, some historians think the missions brought civilization to the natives and helped them get used to a European way of life that would later be thrust on them. These historians point out that at least the mission system included the Native Americans in the development of Alta California. The fathers hoped that the Native Americans would marry the Spanish colonists and become part of the new society. Other countries, such as Great Britain, did not have a plan to include Native Americans. Instead, they just drove them away.

The missions had a large influence on the lives of Native Americans, and on the development of California. That past cannot be undone. Now the **controversy** lies in how the story is told.

This map shows the locations of California's 21 missions and the years in which they were established. Nine of them were founded by Father Serra.

CALIFORNIA
MISSIONS

Sonoma (1823)
San Rafael (1817)
SAN FRANCISCO
Dolores (1776)
San Jose (1797)
Santa Clara (1777)
Santa Cruz (1791)
San Juan Bautista (1797)
Carmel (1770)
El Camino Real
Soledad (1791)
San Antonio (1771)
San Miguel (1797)
San Luis Obispo (1772)
La Purisma (1787)
Santa Ines (1804)
Santa Barbara (1706)
San Buenaventura (1782)
San Fernando (1797)
LOS ANGELES
San Gabriel (1771)
San Juan Capistrano (1776)
San Luis Rey (1798)
San Diego (1769)

PACIFIC OCEAN

Majorca

Balearic
Islands

1713: Miguel José Serra, later known as Father Junípero Serra, is born on November 24, in Petra, Majorca.

1729: Miguel begins his study to become a Franciscan priest in Palma, the capital of Majorca.

1737: Miguel takes his vows and becomes a Franciscan priest. He changes his name to Junípero Serra.

1749: Father Serra sails to Mexico. He arrives in Veracruz on December 6 and begins his walk to Mexico City.

1750: Father Serra arrives in Mexico City on January 1. He begins studying to become a missionary.

In May, Father Serra is assigned to work with the Pame Indians in the Sierra Gorda mountains north of Mexico City.

1758: Father Serra is called back to Mexico City. He spends the next nine years as a traveling missionary in the area.

1767: Father Serra is appointed president of all the Baja missions.

1768: Father Serra goes to Baja to take charge of the missions.

1769: Father Serra founds the first California mission, San Diego de Alcalá, on July 16.

1770: The two Monterey expeditions leave San Diego. Father Serra goes by sea, and Portolá leads the land party.

1771: Father Serra founds Mission San Antonio de Pádua on July 14.

He founds Mission San Gabriel Arcángel on September 8.

1772: Father Serra founds Mission San Luis Obispo on September 1.

On October 20, he begins his journey to Mexico City to petition Viceroy Bucareli to help the missions.

1775: Juan Bautista de Anza arrives in San Gabriel with some 240 settlers. They are the first group of colonists to make the difficult overland journey from Mexico.

1776: Father Serra founds Mission San Francisco de Asis on October 9.

Mission San Juan Capistrano is founded on November 1.

1777: Mission Santa Clara de Asis is founded on January 12.

1782: Father Serra founds Mission San Buenaventura on March 31.

1784: Father Serra dies at Mission San Carlos Borromeo de Carmelo on August 28.

baptized (BAP-tyzd) When someone is baptized, he or she goes through a ceremony with a priest to become officially a Christian. Miguel's parents had him baptized as soon as they could so that he would be a Catholic.

confirm (kun-FIRM) When a priest confirms someone, he admits the person formally to membership in the Church. Father Serra had to get special permission from the Pope to confirm Native Americans.

controversy (KON-truh-ver-see) A controversy is an ongoing argument among many people about a particular subject such as how the story of the California missions is told.

convert (kun-VERT) To convert someone means to make that person change from one religion to another. Priests from Spain converted many Native Americans to Christianity.

council of elders (KOWN-sul of EL-derz) A council of elders is a group of the oldest and most respected members of a community. Native Americans solved many of their arguments by letting a council of elders make decisions.

dedication (ded-ih-KAY-shun) When someone has dedication to something, he or she is willing to spend a lot of time and effort on it. People admired Father Serra's dedication to his plan to build missions in California.

missionary (MIH-shun-eh-ree) A missionary goes to a faraway land to teach people about his or her religion in the hope of converting them. Father Serra was a missionary who believed the Native Americans would be better off if they became Catholic.

missions (MIH-shunz) Missions are religious centers built by Spanish missionaries who came to the Americas to convert Native Americans to Christianity. Father Serra established nine missions in California.

peninsula (pen-IN-soo-luh) An area of land that juts out into the sea. Baja California is a peninsula in the Gulf of Mexico.

presidio (preh-SID-ee-oh) A presidio is a fort built for protection against attack. Serra's men built presidios along with the missions to protect them from attack.

processions (pro-SEH-shunz) A procession is a large group of people all walking together, perhaps in a line, as though in a parade. Sometimes religious ceremonies involve processions that go to a particular place together.

sermons (SER-munz) Sermons are speeches related to religion that priests give in churches. Father Serra was a good speaker and gave interesting sermons.

Books

Ansary, Mir Tamim. *California Indians.* Chicago: Heinemann Library, 2000.

Arnold, Caroline. *Stories in Stone: Rock Art Pictures by Early Americans.* Clarion Books, 1996.

Brower, Pauline. *Missions of the Inland Valleys.* Minneapolis, Minn.: Lerner Publications, 1996.

Dolan, Edward F., Jr. *Famous Builders of California.* New York: Dodd Mead & Co., 1987.

Genet, Donna. *Father Junípero Serra: Founder of the California Missions.* Springfield, N.J.: Enslow Publishers, Inc., 1996.

Van Steenwyk, Elizabeth. *The California Missions.* New York: Franklin Watts, 1995.

Web Sites

Visit our Web page for lots of links about Father Junípero Serra and the California Missions: *http://www.childsworld.com/links.html*

Note to parents, teachers, and librarians: We routinely monitor our Web links to make sure they're safe, active sites.

Sources Used by the Author

Barton, Bruce Walton. *The Tree at the Center of the World.* Santa Barbara, Calif.: Ross-Erikson Publishers, 1980.

Bean, Walton, and James J. Rawls. *California: An Interpretive History.* New York: McGraw-Hill, 1988.

Brower, Pauline. *Missions of the Inland Valleys.* Minneapolis, Minn.: Lerner Publications Co., 1996.

Genet, Donna. *Father Junípero Serra, Founder of the California Missions.* Springfield, N.J.: Enslow Publishers, Inc., 1996.

Reisenberg, Felix, Jr. *The Golden Road.* New York: McGraw-Hill, 1962.

Alaska, 13
Alta California, 12, 13
de Anza, Captain Juan Bautista, 27

Baja California, 13
Bucareli, Antonio, 26

Carlos III, king of Spain, 13
Camino Real, El, 27, 32
Carmel, 21, 30

Fages, Commander Pedro, 20–21, 22,
  24, 26
Father Sitjar, 23

Majorca, Spain, 6–8
Mexico City, 9, 10, 11, 13, 24
Mission Carmel, 21, 28
Mission San Antonio de Pádua, 23
Mission San Buenaventura, 30
Mission San Diego de Alcalá, 16–17
Mission San Francisco de Asis, 26, 28
Mission San Gabriel Arcángel, 23–24,
  27
Mission San Juan Capistrano, 29
Mission San Luis Obispo de Tolosa,
  23, 24
Mission San Luis Rey, 24
Mission Santa Clara de Asis, 30
Monterey, 16, 18, 19, 23, 29

de Neve, Felipe, 28

Palóu, Father Francisco, 8, 9, 10, 28,
  31, 33
Pame Indians, 10–11
de Portolá, Gaspar, 14–15, 16, 18–20

Salinian language, 23
San Diego, 14, 16–17, 19, 32, 34
San Francisco, 20, 26–28, 29, 32
scurvy, 16, 18
Serra, Junípero
  birth, 6
  death, 31
  journey to Americas, 9
  journey to California, 14–16
  in Mexico, 10–13
  schooling, 8
Serra, Margarita and Antonio, 7